Sharing in One Bread

The Easter Enigma

The Pattern of Matins and Evensong

Meet the Prayer Book

Experiment in Worship

The Churchman's Companion
(with D. W. Cleverley Ford,
D. N. Sargent, and Reginald Cant)

Declaring the Faith: The Printed Word
(with Dewi Morgan)

Crisis for Confirmation (editor)

MICHAEL PERRY

Archdeacon of Durham

Sharing in One Bread

HOLY COMMUNION
SERIES THREE

SPCK · LONDON · 1973

First published 1973 by SPCK
Holy Trinity Church, Marylebone Road
London, NW1 4DU

SBN 281 02716 1

Printed in Great Britain by
William Clowes & Sons Ltd.,
London, Colchester and Beccles

To

RONALD JASPER

as a token of appreciation of his work
and that of the Church of England
Liturgical Commission

Contents

Acknowledgements

This is a personal, not an official, commentary on and companion to the Series Three Order for Holy Communion. I hope it will be of use to those encountering this service for the first time—church councillors, congregations, confirmation candidates, and others. It could easily have been very much longer, but then the price would have prevented the wide circulation at which it aimed. Those who want to do further reading on the subject can turn to the books listed on page 79. Canon R. C. D. Jasper has been most helpful in reading an early draft of this book and discussing it in detail. I hope I have benefited from his friendly advice and criticism, and rightly interpreted the mind of the Church of England Liturgical Commission.

Some years ago Messrs Hodder and Stoughton published a book of mine called *The Pattern of Matins and Evensong*; a few sentences from this have been copied into the present volume, and a good many more may be found here in re-worked form. I am grateful for permission to make use of my earlier writing in this way. When the Second Series Holy Communion was first authorized, the SPCK issued an illustrated booklet with the title *Experiment in Worship*, for which I provided the commentary. *Sharing in One Bread* can be thought of in some sense as a revision and expansion of that, and incorporates (though not often without considerable alteration) a great deal of that publication. Quotations from the New Testament are taken from the New English Bible, second edition © 1970, by permission of Oxford and Cambridge University Presses; those from the Psalms are taken from the Jerusalem Bible, © 1966, 1967, 1968 by Darton, Longman & Todd Ltd and Doubleday & Company Inc., by permission of the publishers. I wish to thank Dacre

Press: A. & C. Black Ltd for allowing me to make two quotations from *The Shape of the Liturgy* by Dom Gregory Dix, and the St Andrew Press for a quotation from *The Gospel of St Matthew* in the *Daily Study Bible* by William Barclay.

MICHAEL PERRY

Durham, July 1972

Sharing in One Bread

One April evening, a young Galilean sat down to supper with his companions. He knew quite well that he had made enemies and that in another part of the town they were planning his death; he had a shrewd suspicion that the end could not be far away. At that meal he did something very simple and said something very unusual, intending that in the future his friends should be able to remember him by it. The amazing thing is that, threescore generations later, he still has his friends—vastly more now than then—and that they still remember him in the same way. Innumerable gallons of ink have been used up in the attempt to plumb the depths of meaning locked up in those simple actions and unusual words; which goes to show that, at the very least, that young man was a man of exceptional genius. His friends, of course, claim much more than that about him. That is one reason why this book has been written.

'The Lord Jesus', wrote Paul (and in writing it claimed that he had the tradition from the Lord himself) 'on the night of his arrest, took bread and, after giving thanks to God, broke it and said: "This is my body, which is for you; do this as a memorial of me." In the same way, he took the cup after supper, and said: "This cup is the new covenant sealed by my blood. Whenever you drink it, do this as a memorial of me."' (1 Cor. 11. 24f). But the Lord Jesus gave no detailed directions as to how his friends were to 'do this', so that, as the ages have passed, his command has been interpreted in a multiplicity of ways from the simplest of shared meals to the most splendid ceremonious pomp. 'Was ever another command so obeyed?' asked Dom Gregory Dix in his study *The Shape of the Liturgy*, and answered his question by listing some of the circumstances

in which men have 'done this' in response to those words
of the Lord Jesus:

> For century after century, spreading slowly to every con-
> tinent and country and among every race on earth, this
> action has been done, in every conceivable human cir-
> cumstance, for every conceivable human need from
> infancy and before it to extreme old age and after it, from
> the pinnacles of earthly greatness to the refuge of fugi-
> tives in the caves and dens of the earth. Men have found
> no better thing than this to do for kings at their crowning
> and for criminals going to the scaffold; for armies in
> triumph or for a bride and bridegroom in a little country
> church; for the proclamation of a dogma or for a good
> crop of wheat; for the wisdom of the Parliament of a
> mighty nation or for a sick old woman afraid to die; ...
> tremulously, by an old monk on the fiftieth anniversary
> of his vows; furtively, by an exiled bishop who had hewn
> timber all day in a prison camp near Murmansk; gor-
> geously, for the canonisation of S. Joan of Arc—one
> could fill many pages with the reasons why men have
> done this, and not tell a hundredth part of them.[1]

Our own Church of England has its place in this great roll
of honour—and our people, too, have obeyed the Lord's
command in many ways and over many centuries. Think of
St Cuthbert in his remote hermitage on the Farne Islands,
of Becket in his cathedral at Canterbury, of Charles I on
the morning of his execution, of yourself in your parish
church perhaps this very morning—all taking part in something which has been done (again in the words of Dom
Gregory) 'week by week and month by month, on a
hundred thousand successive Sundays, faithfully, unfail-
ingly, across all the parishes of christendom'.

Christians have always set great store by the service of
the Holy Communion, and have always wanted to make

1. Gregory Dix, *The Shape of the Liturgy* (Dacre Press 1945),
p. 744.

sure that the way in which it has been celebrated should mirror men's increasing understanding of the depths of truth within it. The history of the continuous process of change in the words of the service and the different ways in which it has been carried out is therefore the history not only of how the People of God have prayed over the centuries but how they have understood and interpreted the words and actions of Jesus at the Last Supper. A great deal of re-thinking and change took place in England between 1548 and 1662, by means of which the Church in this country replaced the Roman rite in the Latin tongue by the Anglican rite in the English language. The permanent liturgical result of those centuries of ferment is to be found in the Book of Common Prayer of 1662 which has been treasured by so many generations of devout Anglicans.

But there are many differences between the world of 1662 and our own day. In view of them, ought we to reconsider the way in which we clothe our continuing obedience to that command of Jesus?

Language has changed. Even Cranmer, who more than any other single individual was responsible for the first English Prayer Book, recognized the need for continual review of words and expressions. He once wrote that what had been everyday speech a few centuries before his time was by then 'such antique manners of writing and speaking, that few men now been able to read and understand them'.[1] The same is true today. Look up these words in the 1662 Holy Communion service, and see how their common meaning has changed over three centuries: confess, creatures, curate, divers, fulfilled, hearty, meet, reasonable. But it is not only a matter of the *meanings* of words. Expressions which could be sincerely used in the General Confession in 1662 now sound melodramatic, and sentences nowadays are shorter and less involved than they used to be.

1. *Cranmer's Selected Writings*, edited by C. S. Meyer (SPCK 1961), p 2.

Social conditions have changed. They have altered almost beyond recognition since the times of the first English Prayer Book. Then there was a rigidly hierarchical society in which everybody had his place and almost everybody accepted it. Education was rare and few people could read, even if they could afford to buy books. At that time it made sense to give the parson the dominant part in the service, and have very few places where the people were expected to join in. The people had to say their part of the service phrase by phrase after the minister. (That explains, incidentally, the 'saying after me' of the words just before the General Confession in Morning and Evening Prayer, and the capital letters in the middle of sentences, which were placed there to show the parson how to break things up into phrases for the people to repeat after him.)

Customs have changed. There are fashions in liturgy as much as in everything else. Today we like to involve the people more actively with the priest as together they celebrate the holy mysteries, and share together in one bread. Many of our new churches have been designed to make this more natural.

Liturgical scholarship has not stood still, either. We now know far more than Cranmer ever did about the worship of the earliest Christians, and about the way in which the rite has evolved over the centuries. This does not mean that we must become antiquarians for antiquarianism's sake. Our aim rather is to worship God and obey the command of Jesus in a way which is as full of meaning for twentieth-century Englishmen as their own rite was in their own time for the generations which have gone before us.

All this means that, however much many people may love it and still be able to worship with relevance and understanding through it, the 1662 Book of Common Prayer ought not to be the *only* way of worship for the Church of England. As Humphrey Prideaux wrote about the Prayer Book,

In every age some words that were in use in the former grow obsolete, and some phrases and expressions formerly in grace and fashion through disuse become uncouth and ridiculous; and always to continue these in our Liturgy without correction would be to bring a disparagement upon the whole and expose to contempt the worship of God among us. Besides, there are several things which in one age may conduce to devotion which, through variation of times and circumstances, may not be borne in another; several things which may be the proper matter of prayer at one time, which may not be so in another; and all those things call for alterations and amendments whenever they happen.

His proposal was therefore

I think it absolutely necessary from the above mentioned particulars that it be always at least once in thirty years brought to a review for this purpose.[1]

And that was in 1689! The review which Humphrey Prideaux wanted did not then materialize, and neither did other attempts which were made subsequently. A revision in 1928 which was passed by the Church Assembly failed to secure the approval of Parliament and therefore could not be legally used. But under new legislation, passed in 1965, various alternative and experimental services have been authorized—which explains why this present service is part of 'Series Three'. There have so far been three series of new services. The first is based on the proposals of 1928; the second was first authorized in 1967; and the third begins with this service of Holy Communion.

No congregation is *bound* to use this service. It can only be introduced with the consent of the Parochial Church Council. There may still be places where the attitude is 'Parson knows best' and the PCC are prepared to pass a

---

1. *Anglicanism*, compiled and edited by P. E. More and F. L. Cross (SPCK 1935), pp 184f.

new service 'on the nod' if the Vicar wants it. This is not the most intelligent way to introduce liturgical change. It would be far better if the PCC were first to study the proposed service in some detail—perhaps to see it in action a few times—and to decide only after thought and prayer and study. An informed decision of this kind is of far more value than a blind desire to do the latest thing or to leave it to the parson.

Perhaps this book may be of use to PCC members faced with such a decision about the new service; perhaps it may assist congregations beginning to use Series Three and wanting to worship with the understanding as well as with the spirit; perhaps it may help open up the Holy Communion service to confirmation candidates or the newly-confirmed in parishes which have already decided to use Series Three. I hope so, because all these groups of people have been in mind in the writing of it. If the questions at the end of each division are of any help, use them; if not, they can be ignored.

In this book we shall go through the service section by section, showing that it has an overall shape and pattern and how each section fits into that pattern. Except occasionally, there will be no more about the history of the rite and no comparisons between the new service and what went before it. We shall assume that the service is in use in your church and that you know no other way of celebrating the Holy Communion. Together we will look at Series Three and see what it can tell us about the Lord's command to 'do this in remembrance' of him, and what it means to share through it in one bread.

---

1. Would you expect to gain anything from a knowledge of the history of the Holy Communion service? (See the books listed on page 79 if you want to begin such a study.)

2. What advantages and disadvantages are there in having

many different congregations all using the same form of service?

3. How would you go about preparing your parish for a possible changeover from its present service of Holy Communion to Series Three?

Two in One

There are two parts to the service. The first is called *The Word and The Prayers* and runs from sections 1 to 20. The second (sections 21–45) is *The Communion*. Each part has its focus and its climax. The focal point of the Word and the Prayers is the Bible and the climax comes at the reading of the Gospel, whilst the Communion is focused on the table and comes to its climax when the People of God join together in their common meal. As in all good drama, the final climax is the more important, and very little is left to do after we have reached it.

This point about the two parts of the service can be made through the eye as well as through the ear. The first part—the service of Bible readings and intercessions—does not need a table and need not therefore be conducted from the altar. To show that ministers and congregation belong together and are together involved in the service, the ministers can come in through the congregation and go to their places by the prayer-desk. One of them can carry the Bible and place it solemnly on the place from which the readings are to be given. The table will be bare and no notice will be taken of it. In some churches the first part of the service will be taken from a variety of positions—the readings from the lectern, the sermon from the pulpit, the prayers (which are the prayers of the whole Church, clerical and lay) from the body of the church. In other churches, to move about so constantly during this part of the service may be felt to give it a restless air, and the whole may be taken from a reading-desk either in front of the table, or to one side of it.

When the second part begins, and we are ready to bring up the bread and wine, the ministers can begin to lay the table ready for the meal. Some churches even have a movable table which can be brought into its place in the nave at this point in the service.

In other churches, there may be little room for this sort of visual distinction between the two parts of the service. Not all church buildings can be adapted without spoiling them, and sometimes there is simply no space to do the sort of things described above without creating fussy and unaesthetic clutter. When this is the case, the words of the service will have to bear the whole brunt of showing that the Holy Communion is two services rolled into one.

The rubrics (the printed directions for the conduct of the service) mention a person called the 'president'. This word first appears at section 15 (the intercessions) and is used frequently in the second part of the service. The word 'liturgy' is derived from two Greek words meaning 'the work of the people', and we should never forget that Christian worship is the business of the whole People of God, and that everyone has his 'liturgy' in the Holy Communion service. It cannot be celebrated by a priest alone— he needs a congregation with him, to do their work of worship, their part in the liturgy. The president is the man who presides over the whole service. We first find the term in the works of Justin Martyr, in the second century, where, describing the Eucharist, he says 'When the president has given thanks and the whole congregation has assented, those whom we call deacons give to each of those present a portion of the eucharistized bread and wine and water'; but the idea of everyone having his own 'liturgy' within the service goes back even earlier, to Clement of Rome in the first century. The president acts before God as the chief representative of the people, doing something for which he has been called, chosen, trained, and ordained. On behalf of the congregation he does what Jesus commanded with the bread and wine. And because he is a president to direct it all, not a dictator to impose upon the people, the position he adopts at the table is also significant. In some churches he stands with his back to the people, facing in the same direction as they do, showing that he is one of them and that he stands on the manward side of the table at which God is host. In others he will stand facing the people, looking over the table at them, with his assistants on either side, showing that there is a circle round the Lord's table and that all the Lord's people are gathered together round his board.

But although there are two parts to the service, it would be disastrous if they were unrelated to each other. We cannot properly understand what this Meal is about unless it is put into its context within the whole of God's message to us. Without the Biblical background, the meal could degenerate into a meaningless superstition. But equally, it is no good listening to God's word unless we follow it up by feeding not only upon God's word but upon his very self. That is why the two halves interlock and form a unity. There are two parts—but one service.

Before we go through it in detail, a few words about the language in which the service is written. It is 'contemporary'. But what does this word 'contemporary' mean? 'In everyday use'? But there is more than one kind of language used in everyday life. There is dialect; there is slang; there is the talk of the market street; there is poetry; there is the kind of speaking which is appropriate when addressing a public meeting and highly inappropriate when talking over the breakfast table. Different styles of speech are appropriate to different occasions. What style should we use for a religious service? Some people squirm with embarrassment when they hear God addressed as 'you'. Probably many Jews did so when they heard Jesus speak to God as 'Abba', which is a child's word for his daddy. It could be argued that 'thee' and 'thou' *are* words in contemporary use in the specialized context of liturgy, where they give the appropriate aura of reverence to talk addressed to God. Unfortunately, 'thee'-language is impossible without such words as 'wouldst' and 'didst', which are such a stumbling-block to people who do not know the rules of grammar well enough to move at ease in such language. Churches which have changed over from the 'thee'-form to the 'you'-form (as in New Zealand) claim that the 'you'-form comes to seem natural in a surprisingly short time.

Whether we settle for 'thee' or 'you', we shall never please everybody. Some people believe it is essential not to separate the holy and the profane by a barrier of language, and important that we should emphasize the relevance of religion to daily life by using the same kind of language for both. Other people find security in the thought that they are using words hallowed by centuries of devotion which, like the massive Norman pillars of some great cathedral, speak to them of 'Jesus Christ the same yesterday, today, and for ever'.

In Series Three we use contemporary language—dignified and not slangy; language appropriate to a religious rite of some solemnity and yet not language completely divorced from that of the market street. For certain prayers and texts held in common with other Christian communions, both Roman Catholic and Free Church, we use forms based on those agreed by a body known as the International Consultation on English Texts. The Lord's Prayer (for example) is not the possession of the Church of England alone, and it is a good witness to the essential unity we share with other Christian bodies if we can use the same form of words as they do when we are saying the same prayer. It reminds us that the Church of Christ is larger than our own understanding of the truth of Christ. But change for the sake of change is pointless and some people know the old forms so well that they cannot use new words without a sense of artificiality; or there may be a well-known musical setting which fits the old words but not the new ones. If this is so, then for certain sections of the service (detailed in the introductory notes) we can continue to use the words for which the musical setting was composed, or else the forms in Second Series which have become familiar. Language should lead us to God, and it would be the height of stubborn folly to make people use forms of prayer which rivet their attention on the words and do not allow the soul to pass beyond the words to him of whom they speak.

---

1. If Series Three is to be used in your church, how can the two-fold nature of the Holy Communion service be most clearly indicated?

2. Is there any need to emphasize the structure of the service by actions as well as by words?

3. Ought the service to be in modern language? If so, what *kind* of modern language?

The Word and The Prayers

The Preparation

1 Seasonal sentences.

2 At the entry of the ministers a sentence (section 1) may be used; and a hymn, a canticle, or a psalm may be sung.

3 The minister may say

> The Lord be with you.

All   **And also with you.**

4 The following prayer may be said.

All   **Almighty God,**
to whom all hearts are open,
all desires known,
and from whom no secrets are hid:
cleanse the thoughts of our hearts
by the inspiration of your Holy Spirit,
that we may perfectly love you,
and worthily magnify your holy Name;
through Christ our Lord. Amen.

5 The Kyries may be said.

> Lord, have mercy.
> **Lord, have mercy.**
> Lord, have mercy.

> **Christ, have mercy.**
> Christ, have mercy.
> **Christ, have mercy.**

> Lord, have mercy.
> **Lord, have mercy.**
> Lord, have mercy.

Or the canticle Gloria in Excelsis may be said.

All   **Glory to God in the highest,**
                       and peace to his people on earth.

                       Lord God, heavenly King,
                       almighty God and Father,
                       we worship you, we give you thanks,
                       we praise you for your glory.

                       Lord Jesus Christ, only Son of the Father,
                       Lord God, Lamb of God,
                       you take away the sin of the world:
                       have mercy on us;
                       you are seated at the right hand of the
                       **   Father:**
                       receive our prayer.

                       For you alone are the Holy One,
                       you alone are the Lord,
                       you alone are the Most High,
                       Jesus Christ, with the Holy Spirit,
                       in the glory of God the Father. Amen.

6 The collect of the day.

Words matter. Words on the telephone giving a message
from an absent friend. Words in the newspapers telling us
what is happening on the other side of the world. Words
on the teleprinter making international business possible.
Words at the United Nations keeping nations from war.
Words between friends; words between lovers. Words
make a difference. They do things. They matter.

   This first part of the service centres on God's Word. If
men's words matter, then God's word matters even more.
So we cannot simply crash in and expect to hear God's

word without preparation. The beginning of this service should be rather like an important interview, as you stand at a door waiting for a voice to say 'Come in'. You have mixed feelings. For a start, you are rather nervous, wondering what sort of questions he will ask you, and how much he already knows about you. Yet you are also rather excited. It is a wonderful opportunity, and you must have done well to get short-listed. You are here by special invitation.

There are mixed feelings at the beginning of the Holy Communion service. You are about to keep an appointment with God. You ought to be a bit nervous. He knows all about you. There isn't anything you can keep from him. Yet the appointment is to give thanks—this is what the phrase 'to make Eucharist' means. And your invitation comes from God himself; you are not a gatecrasher. So you should also be rather excited. Your language should be ready to break out into joyful expression. The Preparation (sections 1–6) allows for both these kinds of feeling, for both are proper.

Some sections of the service will be used at every celebration. Others are optional, so that the liturgy can vary— from church to church, or from time to time in the same church. It is not a fixed, static, dead thing, but the expression of the worship of a living Church and a living congregation (after all, we believe in life before death as well as in life after death!). Circumstances are not always the same. Sometimes we may want to emphasize the joyful aspect, at others it may be the aspect of holy fear. We can choose what parts of the Preparation best fit *this* congregation at *this* moment of time. Only one section (6) must always be used.

This is the Collect of the day.[1] Many of the Collects are Cranmer's translations of ancient Latin prayers; some are

1. There will be more than one in Lent and Advent and at various other seasons, or when a lesser saint is being commemorated in an additional Memorial Collect.

his own compositions; others are by later writers, such as John Cosin, Bishop of Durham in the seventeenth century, who was largely responsible for the final form of the 1662 Book of Common Prayer. The Collect is a particular request to God and we pray it, not for ourselves alone, nor even for our own congregation, but on behalf of the whole Church of God. Each Sunday or holy day has its own Collect which helps set the tone of the whole service. The blinding white light of Christian truth needs to be broken down into the colours of the spectrum. There is too much in it for us to concentrate on all of it at the same time. So at Christmas we are particularly aware of the joy coming into the world through Jesus the baby in the manger who was born in the town of David as a Saviour for the whole people; at Passiontide we think of the tree on which that same Jesus hung as he bore our sins that we might die to sin and be healed by his wounds; at Easter we rejoice that he has risen from the dead; and so on. As the years come round, so we enter more and more fully into all the mysteries of the Faith, finding each time (Matt. 13. 52) something old on which to ground our trust in God, and something new to delight and excite us. 'Grow in grace', said the author of 2 Peter (3. 18), and we know that we shall 'never leave growing till the world to come'. Part of the amazing fullness of the Holy Communion is that it can be offered in so many contexts, with so many 'special intentions', and that it can take its especial colour from so many facets of the truth of the Gospel.

There is another Collect in the Preparation, which is for optional use only. It is so well known and loved, however, that it is probable that it will not often be left unsaid when Series Three is used. This is the Collect for Purity (section 4). In it we acknowledge that there is nothing in us which is hidden from God—our innermost hearts and desires, all the secrets we keep even from our closest friends; even the things about ourselves that we have kept hidden from our conscious minds. As the Psalmist said long ago,

Yahweh,[1] you examine me and know me,
you know if I am standing or sitting,
you read my thoughts from far away,
whether I walk or lie down, you are watching,
you know every detail of my conduct.

The word is not even on my tongue,
Yahweh, before you know all about it;
close behind and close in front you fence me round,
shielding me with your hand.
Such knowledge is beyond my understanding,
a height to which my mind cannot attain. (Ps. 139. 1–6)

The idea of coming close to this God will fill us with holy
fear—not the terror of the Unknown God, but reverent
awe before the one who is so great that we can never plumb
his depths and yet so loving as to have invited us to share
in his table. If God is this sort of God, we must ask him to
purify our hearts by his Holy Spirit so that our love for him
may be perfect. Clearly this is more than a lifetime's work;
but it can be begun now. If it is begun, then we shall be
magnifying God's holy Name. Notice, by the way, the
capital N in Name. God's 'Name' is not the word by which
he is known, like Yahweh in the Old Testament. God does
not need a name like that, as though there were a multitude
of gods and we needed to distinguish our own from the rest
by giving him a proper name. 'I am that I am', he said to
Moses (Exod. 3. 14); God is Being itself—Being *him*self.
So 'Name' here is a word describing the very nature and
essence of God himself; and we ask that we may worthily
'magnify' God in his very self. How can we? He is already
so great as to need no help from us. We cannot do anything to make him any greater than he is already. What we
do is to *ascribe* to God some of the greatness that is his by
nature. The difference is not in God but in our idea of him,

---

1. The Old Testament personal name for God, more familiar to
English readers in its mispronounced form 'Jehovah'.

just as a magnifying glass does not alter the size of an
object but only makes it appear larger to us.

> In my heart, though not in heaven,
> I can raise thee.

For many of us it is true that 'our God is too small'. We
need to get a sufficiently big idea of God to worship him.

The Collect for Purity is only one of the sections which
can be added before the Collect of the Day in the Preparation. At the entry of the ministers (section 2) there can
be one or other of the opening sentences given in section 1,
and/or a hymn, a canticle, or a psalm. All of these elements
help to emphasize the appropriate seasonal note which the
Collect will later strike.

Between the two Collects there may be said or sung
either the *Kyries* or the *Gloria in Excelsis* (section 5). 'Lord,
have mercy' (in Greek, *Kyrié, eleison*) is a cry particularly
appropriate to penitential seasons. The fact that we call it
by its Greek name (and in some churches even sing it in
Greek) reminds us that it was a very early part of the
Church's worship, going back to those distant times before
the Church in Western Europe began to use Latin for its
services. It was a cry for mercy to the merciful Lord Christ,
and the phrase was so short that it became the custom to
chant it in three-fold, and then in nine-fold form.

As an alternative to the *Kyries* there may be said or sung
Gloria in Excelsis. This is known by its opening phrase in
Latin, though it was in fact a Greek hymn and its series of
acclamations of praise is characteristic of the ancient
Greek liturgies.

Its opening words, 'Glory to God in the highest', echo
the angels' song heard by the shepherds of Bethlehem when
Christ first came to earth (Luke 2.14). They remind us that
the same body which was born of Mary is about to be made
known to us in bread and wine. Because Christ once came
to earth, he can now no longer leave it. The mystery of the
Incarnation—God made flesh—is no less a mystery than

the mystery of the Holy Communion—God in bread and wine coming continually to this earth and becoming part of our flesh. To realize this ought to fill us with the mixed feelings we spoke of earlier, so that in one breath we can join in the song of the angels and sing of peace and worship and thanks and praise for God's glory, and yet in the very next breath be reminded of ourselves, and ask for mercy lest we be shrivelled by that holy splendour which cannot co-exist with sin.

Our first acclamation was to God the Father, the almighty heavenly King. When we realize what a gulf there is between his holiness and our imperfection, it is to God the Son that we turn, because he takes away the sin of the world, and by becoming man has removed for ever the possibility of that gulf being impassable. But the final word cannot be with ourselves and our unworthiness, so the hymn ends with an ascription of glory to Christ, asserting that the titles which belong to God alone (the Holy One, the Lord, the Most High) belong equally to Jesus Christ and to the Holy Spirit. The Christian faith is in the Trinity in Unity, a dogma which cannot be philosophized into dry tomes, but must be sung as a reality of Christian experience.

How right it is that this hymn is the shape it is! It may be perfectly true that man is a sinner and in a bad way; but that is not the place to begin. Unless a man's eyes have first been opened to the glory of God, he will never know the seriousness of the gap between that dazzling reality and his own dim self. Look how it happened with Isaiah. First the temple vision of the Lord on his throne, high and exalted, and the seraphs with their ceaseless wings and the cries of 'Holy, Holy, Holy'; then, and only then, 'Woe is me! I am lost, for I am a man of unclean lips' (Isa. 6. 1ff). Look how it happened with Peter. First the miraculous draught of fishes; then the realization floods in upon him of a reality greater than himself; *then* he implores Jesus to go away from him, because sin and that reality cannot live together (Luke 5. 1–11). But in every case, once the realization has come, the forgiveness is there and the task given. Isaiah has his message to proclaim, Peter the flock of Christ to tend, we our work for Christ to do. We shall see the same sort of pattern in the Holy Communion service.

---

1. Do you think it a good or a bad idea to have a service with a large number of alternatives or optional sections?

2. Discuss how, by ringing the changes in sections 1–6, you can vary the 'feel' of the beginning of the service.

3. What attitude of mind should we have when approaching God in worship?

The Ministry of the Word

7 Sit

The Old Testament lesson. At the end there may be said

Reader   This is the word of the Lord.

All   **Thanks be to God.**

Silence may be kept.

8 A psalm may be said.

9 The Epistle. At the end there may be said

Reader   This is the word of the Lord.

All   **Thanks be to God.**

Silence may be kept.

10   A canticle, a hymn, or a psalm may be sung.

11   Stand
The Gospel. When it is announced

> All   **Glory to Christ our Saviour.**

At the end the reader says

> This is the Gospel of Christ.

> All   **Praise to Christ our Lord.**

Silence may be kept.

12   Sit
The sermon.

At the end silence may be kept.

13   Stand
The Nicene Creed is said, at least on Sundays and
greater Holy Days.

> All   **We believe in one God,**
> **the Father, the Almighty,**
> **maker of heaven and earth,**
> **of all that is seen and unseen.**
>
> **We believe in one Lord, Jesus Christ,**
> **the only Son of God,**
> **eternally begotten of the Father,**
> **God from God, Light from Light,**
> **true God from true God,**
> **begotten, not made,**
> **one in Being with the Father.**
> **Through him all things were made.**
> **For us men and for our salvation**
> **he came down from heaven;**

by the power of the Holy Spirit
he was born of the Virgin Mary,
   and became man.
For our sake he was crucified under
   Pontius Pilate;
he suffered, died, and was buried.
On the third day he rose again
in fulfilment of the Scriptures;
he ascended into heaven
and is seated at the right hand of the
   Father.
He will come again in glory
to judge the living and the dead,
and his kingdom will have no end.
We believe in the Holy Spirit, the Lord,
   the giver of life,
who proceeds from the Father and the
   Son.
With the Father and the Son he is
   worshipped and glorified.
He has spoken through the Prophets.
We believe in one holy catholic and
   apostolic Church.
We acknowledge one baptism for the
   forgiveness of sins.
We look for the resurrection of the dead,
and the life of the world to come. Amen.

The Church is in the world to give out God's word to the world. But before it can proclaim that word, it has to hear it, so—at the climax of the first part of the service—the People of God place themselves under the Word of God in the House of God, and listen to what God has to say to them. God speaks to his people in the Bible and through the sermon, and they sum up their faith in the Creed.

There can be three Bible readings (sections 7, 9, and 11); sometimes there are only two. The reading from the Gospels (section 11) is the one which is never missed out. In it we hear about the earthly life of the Word made flesh, who gave us his flesh to eat and who instituted the Holy Communion as a means of making himself part of us and we a part of him (as St Athanasius said, he was made man so that man might become divine). The Gospel reading therefore is surrounded by special honour. We sit for the others, but stand for this; and in many churches, the reader will come out from his place and the Gospel book will be carried out towards the people, often flanked by assistants bearing lighted candles, to symbolize Christ the Light of the World.

There is more than one possible course of readings, and individual churches using Series Three have freedom of choice of which to accept. The 1662 Prayer Book contains a series of epistles and gospels for Sundays and major Saints' days. Series 1 added an Old Testament lesson, taken from the eucharistic lectionary of the Anglican Church in India. Series Three incorporates a completely new scheme of readings which was worked out by representatives of many Churches in the Joint Liturgical Group, so that when this lectionary is used, we can feel that even though separated Christians worship apart from each other, they can at least be united in the study and proclamation of the same portions of Scripture on the same Sunday.

The Old Testament reading (section 7) is from the Bible which Jesus loved and knew and from which he prayed. To listen to it reminds us that Jesus did not burst upon a world totally unprepared for him. Some of the Old Testament (the ritual parts of the Law of Moses, for example) have been superseded by the New; but there is much which points forward to the New Testament (such as the prophecies of Messiah's coming), much which acts as background to the New Testament and without which it would be hard to make sense of the New Testament, and very much which is of permanent value and without which the Christian Church would be intolerably impoverished. If the Church were to lose contact with the Old Testament it would have lost contact with the roots of its faith. The introductory notes to the service therefore suggest that when the Series Three lectionary is used but there are only two readings, the Old Testament should be read in preference to the Epistle at least during the nine weeks before Christmas, that being the time when we prepare to celebrate the coming of Christ by listening to the narratives of the creation of the world, the fall of man, the choice of Israel, and the prophecies of a coming Messiah.

After each of the first two lessons there may be a proclamation by the reader—'This is the word of the Lord', to which the people respond by thanking God. Similarly, they ascribe glory and praise to Christ as Saviour and Lord before and after the Gospel. 'Gospel' means 'good news' and it is right to be joyful when we hear it.

'This is the word of the Lord', says the reader after Old Testament and Epistle (sections 7 and 9). What does this mean? It means that when we listen to the Bible we can hear God speaking to us. We *can*; sometimes we don't. Sometimes we don't because we are inattentive, but at other times it is because what was a genuine revelation of the nature or purpose or will of God to people in one epoch of history no longer speaks in the same way to us who live in a very different world from that of Biblical Palestine and who think in very different ways. Man's ideas about God have deepened or been refined over the centuries, and we are sometimes offended at what seems to us to be primitive or unworthy or simply untrue. 'This is the word of the Lord' does not mean that the words through which we can hear the Word are infallible or that they cannot be bettered; it *does* mean that we should take these words very seriously indeed because God once used them to speak to a people and he has used them time and time again to speak afresh to men in succeeding centuries. Before dismissing a reading as irrelevant, therefore, we should first make quite sure that the fact that it does not speak to us is its fault and not ours. The sermon can often help to pierce that opaque barrier which the centuries have created and which makes it hard for us to overhear God speaking to us as we read how he spoke to the men of the Bible. That is what the sermon is for, and why the preacher has been trained in the arts of translation and interpretation and the application of the scripture to the present day.

God speaks. But in this rushed world of continual noise, when we cannot even go to the supermarket without hearing background piped music, it is so easy to let sounds go into our ears without *really* listening to them. It would be tragic if when God spoke we were similarly inattentive. In any case, the things he has to say to us are so important that we need time to let them slowly and quietly sink in. The rubric (sections 7, 9, 11, and 12) suggests that we keep silence after each reading and after the sermon. Unless it is a Family Eucharist with a lively set of toddlers, there is much to be said for taking this suggestion up. The silence needs to be not a few seconds only, but long enough to allow people to ponder what they have heard, and to store up God's message in their hearts.

Another way of ensuring that the readings strike home is to separate them by words of commentary. The Old Testament lesson may be followed (section 8) by a psalm chosen to emphasize some aspect of the reading, and the Epistle (section 10) by a canticle or hymn or psalm. An Appendix to the service (not printed in this book) gives a suggested choice of psalms and canticles. If there is a hymn at section 10, it should be one which fits in with the theme of the readings and helps to underline their message.

The sermon (section 12) follows immediately upon the readings, because it is an integral part of the ministry of God's word. Whenever possible there ought to be a sermon—even as short a sermon as sixty seconds—commenting upon the readings, opening them up to the congregation, explaining and expounding them, bringing their message out from the past and relating it to the needs and opportunities of the present, renewing and deepening our understanding of the word God has spoken. Too many people think of the sermon as the preacher's chance of expressing his own private views and airing his own private prejudices without fear of contradiction. It is true that he should have thought about the sermon and prayed over it and prepared it until his message is indeed a part of himself and expresses his own deepest convictions; but it should not be *his* word. It is his opportunity of obeying the charge given to him at the moment of his ordination, where he was bidden to be 'a faithful dispenser of the word of God'. *God* should be able to speak to the congregation through the sermon, as he does through the readings. The preacher who realizes this will not be made self-opinionated and dogmatic, but very humble; and the congregation will be reverently and expectantly receptive. The preacher will pray that his hearers will soon forget whatever in the sermon is his and not his Lord's, and that they will treasure in their hearts whatever in it is of the Lord—remembering, not him who told it them, but God alone.

When they have listened to God's word in Bible and sermon, and silently let it sink in, the people rise to their feet again to recite the Creed (section 13). Here we respond to God's word and sum up all that is essential in the faith which is found in the Bible and has been proclaimed in the sermon. The Creed therefore fittingly closes The Ministry of the Word and is a proper part of it.

We cannot concentrate on every aspect of the faith every time we come to the Eucharist, but it is right that we should often be reminded that it *is* a coherent whole, and that all of it matters. Otherwise it is so easy to fix only upon those parts of the faith which we think we can understand, or which are congenial to us, and to ignore the rest. This does not mean that the Creed is an essential part of *every* celebration of the Holy Communion, but it does mean that it ought to be there at least on Sundays and greater holy days. These are festival days of Christian rejoicing; the Creed is a shout of joy and Christians are men of joy who know what God is like. At the very centre of their lives is the basic certainty that God is in control of the world and of their destiny.

In the Creed the Church commits herself to the Word, declares that she really believes what God has shown her of himself, and offers back to him all her understanding of the truth about him. Yes—the *Church* does all this. The Creed is primarily the Church's creed, and only secondly the creed of the individuals who belong to the Church. In Series Three we use the original form of the Creed, which was in the first person plural—'We believe'. The Creed is not the statement of a collection of individuals all standing up and saying that each happens to believe in the same set of unrelated statements. It sets forth the faith of the Church and tells us that Christianity is something objective. We can take it or leave it, but we cannot pick and choose as though the Creed were a sort of spiritual hors d'oeuvres trolley where a man can take a bit of this tasty-looking morsel but decide to leave the plateful of that for somebody else because he doesn't think he can stomach it. Christianity is the faith of the Church, whole and objective and definable. You can disagree with it (either as a whole or on particular details) but you cannot subtract things from it or add things to it and still call it Christianity. A person who aligns himself wholeheartedly with the faith of the Church will want to translate the 'We believe' into 'I believe'.

But what of those many people who find it impossible to do this? People who honestly and sincerely want to attach themselves to the Church but who cannot accept the Creed in its entirety? Are they debarred from coming to church or from joining in the Creed? By no means. Let them use it, and say as they do, 'This is the faith of the Church of which

I want to be a sincere member. It may not be, in every detail, my own personal faith. But I want to find God within the fellowship of his Church, and I realize that it uses these words to express its faith in him'. Faith comes more easily to some people than to others, and (unless there is something very much the matter) our understanding of God will deepen as we enter more fully into the Christian life. Perhaps, as this happens, more and more of 'we believe' can be expressed by the individual in terms of 'I believe'. But perhaps not. Our confession of faith is bound to be partial, very often stumbling, sometimes even doubting. Yet we can say, as a man in desperate need once said to Jesus (Mark 9. 24), 'I have faith; help me where faith falls short', and we can use the form of words which expresses the truth as God has made it known to countless Christians through the ages, realizing that now we know in part, but that the time will come when, beyond this present life, we shall know as perfectly as we are known.

---

1. How often ought the Old Testament to be read at the Eucharist?

2. Is it desirable (or practicable) to have periods of silence during church services?

3. What ought the sermon to be about?

4. Is a sermon still the best way of linking the Bible readings with contemporary concerns?

The Prayers

14 Banns of marriage and other notices may be published; the offerings of the people may be collected; and a hymn may be sung.

15 Intercessions and thanksgivings are offered by the president or by some other person. These may be introduced by biddings.
It is not necessary to include specific subjects in any section of the following prayer.
The set passages may also follow one another as a continuous whole, without the versicles and responses.

Minister Let us pray for the Church and for the world; and let us thank God for his goodness.
Almighty God, our heavenly Father, who promised through your Son Jesus Christ to hear us when we pray in faith:
We give thanks for / we pray for
the Church throughout the world . . .
our own Church, our diocese and bishop . . .
any particular work of the Church . . .

Silence may be kept.

Strengthen your Church to carry forward the work of Christ; that we and all who confess your Name may unite in your truth, live together in your love, and reveal your glory in the world.

Lord, in your mercy

All **Hear our prayer.**

_____

We give thanks for / we pray for
the nations of the world . . .
our own nation . . .
all men in their various callings . . .

Silence may be kept.

Give wisdom to all in authority,
especially Elizabeth our Queen; direct
this nation and all nations in the ways
of justice and of peace; that men may
honour one another, and seek the
common good.

Lord, in your mercy

All   **Hear our prayer.**

We give thanks for / we pray for
the local community . . .
our families and friends . . .
particular persons . . .

Silence may be kept.

Give grace to us, our families and
friends, and to all our neighbours in
Christ; that we may serve him in one
another, and love as he loves us.

Lord, in your mercy

All   **Hear our prayer.**

We pray for
the sick and the suffering . . .
those who mourn . . .
those without faith . . ,

We give thanks and pray for
all who serve and relieve them . . .

Silence may be kept.

Comfort and heal all those who suffer
in body, mind, or spirit; give them
courage and hope in their troubles; and
bring them the joy of your salvation.

Lord, in your mercy

All   **Hear our prayer.**

We commemorate
the departed especially . . .

Silence may be kept.

We commend all men to your unfailing
love, that in them your will may be
fulfilled; and we rejoice at the faithful
witness of your saints in every age,
praying that we may share with them in
your eternal kingdom.

Lord, in your mercy

All   **Accept these prayers**
for the sake of your Son,
our Saviour Jesus Christ. Amen.

16 The Minister may say the Commandments and
silence may be kept after the responses ; or the
Summary of the Law may be said.[1]

17 Minister   God so loved the world that he gave his
only Son, Jesus Christ, to save us from
our sins, to be our advocate in heaven,
and to bring us to eternal life.

1. The Commandments and the Summary of the Law appear on
pp 42–4.

Let us therefore confess our sins, in
penitence and faith, firmly resolved to
keep God's commandments and to live
in love and peace with all men.

Or he says one or more of these sentences:

Hear the words of comfort our Saviour
Christ says to all who truly turn to him.

Come to me, all who labour and are
heavy-laden, and I will give you rest.

God so loved the world that he gave his
only Son, that whoever believes in him
should not perish but have eternal life.

Hear what St Paul says.

This saying is true and worthy of full
acceptance, that Christ Jesus came
into the world to save sinners.

Hear what St John says.

If anyone does sin, we have an
advocate with the Father, Jesus Christ
the righteous; and he is the expiation
of our sins.

After which he says:

Let us therefore confess our sins, in
penitence and faith, firmly resolved to
keep God's commandments and to live
in love and peace with all men.

18 Kneel

Silence may be kept.

All **Almighty God, our heavenly Father,
we have sinned against you and against our
 fellow men,
in thought and word and deed,
in the evil we have done
and in the good we have not done,
through ignorance, through weakness,
through our own deliberate fault.
We are truly sorry and repent of all our
 sins.
For the sake of your Son, Jesus Christ,
 who died for us,
forgive us all that is past;
and grant that we may serve you in newness
 of life
to the glory of your Name. Amen.**

19 President Almighty God, who forgives all who
truly repent, have mercy upon you,
pardon and deliver you from all your
sins, confirm and strengthen you in all
goodness, and keep you in life eternal;
through Jesus Christ our Lord.

All **Amen.**

20 All may say **We do not presume
to come to this your table, merciful Lord,
trusting in our own righteousness,
but in your manifold and great mercies.
We are not worthy
so much as to gather up the crumbs under
 your table.
But you are the same Lord**

whose nature is always to have mercy.
Grant us therefore, gracious Lord,
so to eat the flesh of your dear Son Jesus
  Christ,
and to drink his blood,
that we may evermore dwell in him,
and he in us. Amen.

We have already, in the Creed, made our response in belief
to the proclamation of God's word which we heard in
readings and sermon; but there is another response which
is equally natural and equally essential, and that is our
response in prayer for the needs of the world God loves.
God acted in Christ because of the sin of the world, and as
we are a part of that world and share in its imperfections,
the prayers lead naturally on to a call to repentance and
the declaration of God's forgiveness. In the enabling
power of that forgiveness we go on to the second part of
the service and celebrate the Holy Communion.

The confession and absolution therefore is the hinge of
the rite, arising naturally out of the first part and leading
on to the second. And the position of the confession within
the rite is significant. As we noticed (page 19 above) when
we were thinking about the *Gloria in Excelsis*, we should
never begin with man and his sin. If we begin with God and
his word and his glory, the realization of our sin should
come unbidden as the dazzling brightness of his revelation
throws the darkness of our shadows into even starker
relief.

The two essential sections in this division of the service
are the intercessions and thanksgivings (15) and the confession with its introduction and the absolution (17–19).

In section 15 we pray for the Church and the world. It is
no good leaving the world at the church door and shutting
it out whilst the service goes on. God is interested in the
world outside. He made it. He cares for it. He came to die

for it. He has plans for it. It is our business to make our prayers no less wide than God's own love. Therefore we pray—within the Holy Communion service, in the most solemn and religious act of the Christian faith—not only for the Church, but for the world which has no use for the Church.

Linked with intercessions, there are thanksgivings. The very word 'Eucharist' means 'thanksgiving'. Someone once told Dr Johnson that he had tried to be a philosopher, but cheerfulness kept breaking in. Christians should find that thankfulness for all God's mercies should keep breaking in at every point in their lives and prayers and church services.

The congregation is bidden to pray for Church and world, and to thank God for his goodness, after which the prayer itself follows in five paragraphs.[1] It may be said straight through, without extempore prayer and without versicles and responses; or particular intercessions and thanksgivings (provided that they are briefly expressed) may be inserted in all five places; or this may be done only at a selection of places. Unless the extempore parts are given in the form of biddings to the people, requesting their prayers for specific objects (in which case they should come at the very beginning of the prayer, before the address to almighty God), they are part of the prayer and should be spoken to God in the form 'we pray for . . .' and not to the congregation ('let us pray for . . .').

First we pray for the Church, because we are part of it, and God wishes to use his Church in bringing about his purposes of love for the whole world. This needs strength from God, and so we pray for it; we pray, too, that the Church may show the world a living example of that unity and love of which the world talks so much and knows so

---

1. Permission is granted, in the introductory notes to the service, for the use of the Second Series form of intercessions if it is preferred to the Series Three wording. The comment here is only on Series Three.

little. If that prayer were answered, the Church would indeed be revealing God's glory to the world. Sometimes
there will be cause for particular thankfulness when we see
this happening somewhere; always there will be room for
intercession because in this life we shall never reach perfec-
tion, but only grope towards it.

The world, then, is never out of sight, even when we are
praying for the Church; but in the next paragraph we turn
to it more explicitly. Especially we pray for those in authority in our own and other nations, praying that there may
be that mutual respect between states which will promote
the well-being of all—not only of the vocal and powerful,
but of the minorities and those who in so many countries
are denied that freedom of expression and movement we
here so often unthinkingly take for granted.

In this paragraph we single out our own Queen and this
nation for special mention. Some people do not like this
particularization, which to them smacks of the jingoistic
belief that God has some extraordinary concern for Englishmen which he does not also have for Frenchmen or
Polynesian islanders. They prefer the humility which
thinks of others as more important than ourselves and so
they dislike a prayer which asks for special favours for this
nation and for Elizabeth our Queen. But this is the way, not
of humility, but of folly. Of course God created every race
of man, but he also fixed the limits of their territory (Acts
17. 26)—and this is not to be interpreted as a divine wish
that international boundaries should remain for ever un-
changed, but as an acknowledgement of the manifest fact
that although God has set each of us in a great world, he
has also set us in a small locality where things of lesser
import make up the greater part of our conscious life, and
in families where strong affection and love is shared within
a small circle. That is why, in the third paragraph of this
prayer, we pray and give thanks for those in our own small
world. If a man does not love the brother whom he has
seen, it cannot be that he loves God whom he has not seen
(1 John 4. 20).

There are always people in especial need, and we continue our prayer by including petitions for them, and by praying for (and thanking God for the love and devotion of) those who serve and relieve them. We pray for the sick, the poor, the dispossessed, the unemployed, the refugees, the homeless, the prisoners; for mourners; but also for those who do not know their sickness—the mentally ill and those who, because they have no faith, do not know what they are missing of the knowledge of God's love. All need courage and hope; all need to become aware of the joy of God's salvation—which some people (as Jesus did) will only find through the dark way of suffering.

Finally, our prayers and thanks widen to include all mankind; living and departed, Christians and pagans and those without any faith at all. We rejoice at the faithful witness of the saints and commend all men living and departed to the love of God, asking that he may fulfil his will in them. What that will is, we do not know in detail, particularly for those who have died outside the faith of Christ; but we know that the will of God is just and good and kind, so we can in confidence leave all men in his sure keeping.

All these intercessions and thanksgivings are the prayers of the Church, and the whole congregation is therefore involved in them. This fact may be emphasized by saying the prayers from the body of the church and not from the president's seat, and by inviting members of the congregation to lead the biddings. There must be forethought and careful preparation of this section if the people's response is to be genuine and meaningful, but this is as it should be. Prayer is a serious business. We devalue it if we think we can pray about anything without putting ourselves at God's disposal for the answering of our prayer. It is our duty, therefore, to think carefully beforehand what things we dare pray about, and if we dare not pray about a certain matter, to examine our conscience to find out why.

How naturally we have been brought from a consideration of prayer to thoughts of penitence! As soon as the

intercessions and thanksgivings are over, we come (in
sections 17–19) face to face with the fact of sin and the need
for forgiveness. Sin *is* a fact. We only need to look around
us, at a world of fear and war and mistrust and suspicion,
to see that man in the mass is not man as God made him
and meant him to be. But the frightening thing about it all
is that in the sins of man in the mass we see our own sins
and inadequacies writ large. And so we are driven to confession—a general confession, in which the congregation
becomes the representative of the whole of fallen humanity, and in which the 'we' includes not only those who
confess but those who refuse to confess and those who feel
no need to confess. All mankind is bound together in the
same bundle of humanity, and all need the same cleansing
power of God.

We confess. But where are our thoughts directed as we
do so? We could be looking in on ourselves, thinking of
what *we* have done and the effect our sin is having on *us*.
That is known as remorse. The other reaction is to see what
sin does to other people and to God, and to want to amend
because we cannot bear to hurt God any more. St Paul
distinguished (2 Cor. 7. 10) between the sorrow of the
world that works death and godly sorrow which works repentance unto salvation. In order that we should be peni-
tent rather than remorseful, the invitation to confession
(section 17) directs us towards, not ourselves and our sins,
but God and his love. There are alternative forms. The
briefer one speaks of God so loving the world that he gave
Jesus to save us from our sins, to speak on our behalf before
him in heaven, and to bring us to the life which is life
indeed. The same ideas are expressed at slightly greater
length in the longer introduction which incorporates the
'Words of Comfort'. These Words have been a feature of
the English liturgy since the first English Order of Holy
Communion in 1548. Some people think of 'comfort' as a
word which speaks of a life of lazy ease and luxury—a
comfortable chair or the benefits of central heating. It is

not; it contains the word 'fort' and has the idea of strengthening for service by the assurance that at the bedrock of the Universe is a person who is on our side and who wishes us to be secure in his service. We are bidden therefore to confess our sins, trusting in the mercy of this good God, with a firm resolve to remain in the state of grace to which absolution will bring us, and to walk in God's way in the times ahead.

We confess. Not in exaggerated words, but in a matter-of-fact way which does not prescribe the emotions we should feel, and allows every person in the congregation to feel his own. We look at the past with penitence, recognizing that sin can be caused by weakness and ignorance as well as by deliberate fault, that it consists not only in the evil we have done but in the good we have failed to do, and that it is against God as well as against our fellow-men. We look at the present with security, because of the Words of Comfort. We look at the future with hope, ready to serve God in newness of life to the glory of his Name.

The president then declares that God forgives *all* who truly repent, and applies this universal promise to the members of *this* congregation in particular. (If you are worried about whether your repentance is 'true' repentance qualifying for this promise, your very concern about the matter proves that it is.) But the absolution is not content with talking about *pardon* for our sins; it goes on to talk about deliverance from them (do we not all know how sin sticks, and is as hard to wipe off our souls as glue from our fingers?), about strengthening in all goodness (Jesus once told a story (Matt. 12. 43–5) about a swept room and seven worse devils, and every gardener is ruefully aware of how soon the weeds establish themselves on a newly-cleared patch), and about our being sustained within the life eternal, the life which is life indeed.

These are the invariable elements in this division of the service. For optional use there are the notices, collection, and hymn (section 14), the Ten Commandments or Sum-

mary of the Law (16), and the Prayer of Humble Access
(20). A word on each.

The notices may be given out at any convenient point in
the service, according to the introductory notes; but this is
the point at which it is recommended, in the text of the
service, that they be published. Why give out the notices
here? Does not this intrude something very humdrum into
a sacred rite? No. Worship and life are all of a piece, and
all activities of the People of God are relevant to their
worship. God's Church has no walls. Nothing in which
God's people engage is too secular to be related to the
Eucharist. Notices can include news as well as announce-
ments of forthcoming events; here is the place in the service
where God's family shares its common concerns before
offering them to its heavenly Father in prayer and praise.
And since the notices come immediately before the intercessions and thanksgivings, the prayers should be related
to the notices and the notices can include information
about the subjects of the prayers which are to follow. (This
would at the least prevent the type of prayer which seeks to
inform God what is going on—'Thou knowest, Lord, that
there is to be a meeting of the P.C.C. on Wednesday
week . . .'.) At this point in the service, the collection may
be taken, though it will not be presented at the table until
section 23 (for reasons which will be explained later); and
there is room for a hymn if one is needed.

The Ten Commandments or our Lord's Summary of the
Law (section 16 and appendix) can precede the invitation
to confession. It is only as we begin to realize God's demands upon us that we see just where and how far short
we fall and how much we need confession and absolution. The Commandments of the Old Testament are not,
however, sufficient of themselves as a guide to Christian
behaviour. The Law of the Old Testament is holy and just
and good (Rom. 7. 12), but it needs the revelation of Christ
to deepen, extend, and counterbalance it. So in section 16
each commandment is followed by a New Testament

quotation showing one way in which Christians will want to interpret it. Notice how often this addition turns a negative prohibition into a positive command. To each commandment, the congregation answers 'Amen' to show they accept what it says, and 'Lord, have mercy' to acknowledge how far short they fall of God's demands, and silence may follow each commandment, during which there is an opportunity for self-examination. Alternatively, the Summary of the Law may be used. In it, Jesus himself declares to us what is the essence of the commandments given us in the Old Testament.

Finally, the Prayer of Humble Access (section 20) may follow the absolution and lead us on to the Communion. In it we acknowledge that we are so overwhelmed by God's forgiveness that we can hardly credit it that people like ourselves could come to his most holy sacrament without presumptuousness. We go forward, then, trusting not in ourselves but in God, who will let us eat the flesh and drink the blood of Christ so that his indwelling of us and ours of him may be eternal. This prayer of humility leads us to the place where Christ is to come to earth; and it may remind us of the place where he first came to earth—the Cave of the Nativity in Bethlehem. At the entrance to that cave, there is a very low door, and William Barclay comments that 'there is something beautiful in the symbolism that the church where the cave is has a door so low that all who enter it must stoop to enter. It is supremely fitting that every man should approach the infant Jesus upon his knees'.[1] That same attitude befits all who would see Jesus come to earth again, in bread and wine.

---

1. How can the notices and prayers best be brought into relation with one another?

1. *The Gospel of Matthew*, Vol. 1, p 16. St Andrew Press, 2nd edn 1958.

2. Does this service allow enough place for extempore prayer?

3. Why do the Ten Commandments need interpretation by New Testament quotations?

4. Should there be an act of penitence in every church service?

Appendix

The Commandments

Minister
Our Lord Jesus Christ said, If you love me, keep my commandments: happy are those who hear the word of God and keep it. Hear then these commandments which God has given to his people, and take them to heart.

I am the Lord your God: you shall have no other gods but me.
You shall love the Lord your God with all your heart, with all your soul, with all your mind, and with all your strength.

All **Amen. Lord, have mercy.**

Minister
You shall not make for yourself any idol.
God is spirit, and those who worship him must worship in spirit and in truth.

All **Amen. Lord, have mercy.**

Minister   You shall not dishonour the name
of the Lord your God.
You shall worship him with reverence
and awe.

All   **Amen. Lord, have mercy.**

Minister   Remember the Lord's day and keep
it holy.
Christ is risen from the dead ; set
your minds on things that are above,
not on things that are on the earth.

All   **Amen. Lord, have mercy.**

Minister   Honour your father and mother.
Live as servants of God ; honour all
men ; love the brotherhood.

All   **Amen. Lord, have mercy.**

Minister   You shall not commit murder.
Do not nurse anger against your
brother ; overcome evil with good.

All   **Amen. Lord, have mercy.**

Minister   You shall not commit adultery.
Know that your body is a temple of
the Holy Spirit.

All   **Amen. Lord, have mercy.**

Minister   You shall not steal.
You shall work honestly, and give
to those in need.

All   **Amen. Lord, have mercy.**

Minister   You shall not be a false witness.
Let everyone speak the truth.

All   **Amen. Lord, have mercy.**

Minister	You shall not covet anything which belongs to your neighbour. Remember the words of the Lord Jesus : It is more blessed to give than to receive. Love your neighbour as yourself, for love is the fulfilling of the law.
All	**Amen. Lord, have mercy.**

The Summary of the Law

Our Lord Jesus Christ said : The Lord our God is the only Lord. You shall love the Lord your God with all your heart, with all your soul, with all your mind, and with all your strength. This is the first commandment. The second is this : Love your neighbour as yourself. There is no other commandment greater than these.

Amen. Lord, have mercy.

The Communion

The Peace

21 Stand
President

We are the Body of Christ. In the one Spirit we were all baptized into one body. Let us then pursue all that makes for peace and builds up our common life.

22 The president gives the Peace to the congregation, saying

The peace of the Lord be always with you;

All

And also with you.

Word gives place to action, as we pass to the second part of this two-in-one service. We are human beings, and so often the fine words we say get no further than our tongues. They are easy enough to say, but so hard to do anything about. With God, it is different. He speaks, and in the very speaking, it is done. ('Let there be light; and there *was* light.') He does not only talk about love—he loves us—whatever it costs, even to the giving of the flesh and blood of his only Son for the world's salvation. In the Communion, we are in the part of the service completely controlled by the Word made flesh, where the Word *becomes* action. We have prepared ourselves as best we can through listening and praying and confessing and receiving absolution; now we remember and repeat the four things Jesus did at the Last Supper.

Jesus took, gave thanks, broke, and shared. 'During supper', St Mark tells us (14. 22f), 'he took bread, and having said the blessing he broke it and gave it to them . . . Then he took a cup and having offered thanks to God he gave it to them; and they all drank from it.' So we take bread and wine which we place on the holy Table; we give thanks to God and repeat the words Jesus used on the night he was arrested; we break the bread ready to distribute it; and we share the bread and wine with the whole congregation, as Jesus shared it with his disciples, and as he gives his body and blood for everybody. In Series Three, each of these four actions has a division of the service to itself. But first there is the Peace, and after the four-fold action the final prayer and the dismissal.

The Peace is brief, but it is very significant. The president and congregation stand and face each other. The president makes a brief announcement, and there follows a greeting and a response. That is all; but what a wealth of meaning it contains!

Shalom (pronounced with a short 'a' and a long 'o' and with the accent on the second syllable) is the Hebrew word for 'peace'. It is a standard Hebrew greeting, very like our 'Good morning' or 'Goodbye'. And, just as we so often never stop to think what 'Good morning' or 'God be with ye' ('Goodbye') really means, doubtless many Jews of old used 'Shalom' as their greeting without much thought. But it bears thinking about. It was a word often on the lips of Jesus. We find him instructing a group of followers on how to present the Good News, and saying, 'When you come to any town or village . . . wish the house peace as you enter it, so that, if it is worthy, your peace may descend upon it' (Matt. 10. 11f). We find a huddled group of nervous disciples in an upper room on Easter evening, and of a sudden the Risen Christ is among them. Terrified, they think of ghosts, and the figure says to them, 'Peace be with you' (John 20. 19). Christ came (Eph. 2. 17) 'and proclaimed the good news: peace to you who were far off, and peace to those who were near by'. So the Church has hung on to this conventional Jewish greeting and ensured that it remains full of meaning. Christ is our peace (Eph. 2. 14), and if we are to take his body within our own, we too must be men of peace.

We are forgiven sinners, as the absolution has just reminded us. Through our baptism we are already a part of Christ's body. That body is one; atonement makes men at one with God and also at one with each other. If forgiven sinners are not at one with each other, it is a sign that the atonement has remained only a word and never become a reality. When this is the case, something must be done about it urgently, before the Holy Communion can be meaningfully celebrated. Jesus himself said (Matt. 5. 23f), 'If, when you are bringing your gift to the altar, you suddenly remember that your brother has a grievance against you, leave your gift where it is before the altar. First go and make your peace with your brother, and only then come back and offer your gift.' That is why the Peace comes where it does in the service; it is a sign of reconciliation following an act of penitence and leading on to the laying of our gifts before God's altar.

This is not airy theology. It is understood at least as well in the world outside as in the church itself. Non-Christians *expect* churchmen to be people who know what unity and reconciliation mean, and (to our shame) it often scandalizes them more than it does us when they see churches and congregations which are not at unity; places where there are bickerings and petty jealousies, squabbles over who does the altar flowers or who counts the collection. That we should repel people from Christ's offer of salvation by our dissensions over such trivialities would be laughable if it were not so tragic in its consequences. Alas, it has often been so, and from the earliest days. St Paul had to write in sorrowful anger to Corinth, saying that 'your meetings tend to do more harm than good. . . . When you meet as a congregation you fall into sharply divided groups. . . . The

result is that . . . it is impossible for you to eat the Lord's
Supper' (1 Cor. 11. 17–20). If people who are looking for
Christ cannot find him in the Church, we should be so
ashamed as to do something about it immediately. The
Peace is a warning as well as an encouragement.

That is why, before the Peace, the president reminds the
people (section 21) that peace is not something automatic.
It needs to be worked for, and actively pursued. Similarly,
common life does not come into being simply by herding a
group of people together and telling them to say the same
prayers. It needs to be built up. But it can be done if God's
peace is with us, and so that Peace is given and returned
(section 22) in the salutation and response.

There is an ancient custom going back at least as far as
the second century, and growing in popularity in churches
all over the world today, in which the congregation shows
its unity as the Body of Christ by passing the Peace in the
form of a kiss or handshake or handclasp from the president to his assistants and thence round the whole congregation. But whether the Peace is symbolized in this way, or
whether the president and people simply stand and face
each other and—out loud and with real conviction—wish
each other the Peace of the Lord, this is a fitting way in
which to approach the altar to which we ought only to go
if (so far as lies in *us*) we are in love and charity with all
men, and particularly with those in whose company we
come together to the Holy Communion.

---

1. Ought we ever to come to the service without receiving
Communion?

2. In what ways might the Peace be enacted as well as
being said?

The Taking of the Bread and Wine

23 A hymn may be sung, and the offerings of the people may be collected and presented.

24 The bread and wine are brought to the holy table and this sentence may be used:

> **Yours, Lord, is the greatness, the power, the glory, the splendour, and the majesty; for everything in heaven and on earth is yours.**
> **All things come from you, and of your own do we give you.**

25 The president takes the bread and wine.

At last the time has come for the scene to move to the holy table. All the service so far could have been done without a table and without being followed by a meal. Indeed, it is possible to use Series Three as a service without communion, in which case it will be taken as far as section 19 (the absolution) after which the minister will add the Lord's Prayer, the General Thanksgiving, and any other prayers he thinks suitable, and the service will end with the Grace. But this will not be usual. Most often, at this point in the service, the table will be prepared for the Communion.

The collection may have been taken at another point in the service. In some churches the congregation place their offerings in the plate as they enter the building; in others, the collection will be taken at section 14, after the notices and before the intercessions. But at whatever point the collection is made, if it is to be presented at the table, this will normally be done at section 23, just before the bread and wine are brought there.

The bread and wine may be placed on the table without words or ceremony. In many churches, however, when everything is ready, lay representatives of the congregation come up to the table from the body of the church with the people's offerings and the bread and wine. Whilst this is happening, a hymn may be sung; but the rubrics suggest (by putting the hymn in section 23 and the bringing up of the elements as section 24) that it is better to perform this action in silence, after the hymn if there has been one. This certainly adds point and impressiveness to the procession. When the bread and wine have been received, sentences from 1 Chron. 29. 11 and 14 may be said. The words are those attributed to King David—his prayer of praise and joy and blessing when he asked God to accept the offerings of himself and his people for the building of the temple which Solomon his son was to complete.

One way of arranging the offertory is for the president's assistants to come to the table and lay the cloth on it at the close of the hymn. The representatives of the people then come up, and the assistants, facing the congregation and in full view, accept the alms, take sufficient bread and place it on the paten or in the ciborium, and fill the chalice from the cruet or bottle. All this is so that the people may see what is being done and identify themselves with the actions. The money represents their work and their offerings to be used in God's service, and the bringing up of the bread and wine reminds us that in the Communion we offer our whole self, soul and body, to God. As St Augustine once said, 'There are *you*, upon the altar'; you, a crumb of the bread; you, a drop in the chalice.

Ceremonies like the offertory procession are an attempt to use 'eye-gate' as well as 'ear-gate' and to worship God through meaningful action as well as by words. When a play is performed, it is the producer's business to take the words of the dramatist and arrange the staging and the actions so that they best express what he had in mind. We are engaged in something more important than a play when we celebrate the Holy Communion. It is at least as important in this case that the 'staging' and the actions should help express the meaning of the words and the shape of the service.

After this, the president himself comes to the table and 'takes' the bread and wine, performing the first of the four actions of the Communion. The bringing of the elements to the table and the taking are two distinct and separate acts (section 24 and section 25). At the Last Supper the bread and the wine were already on the table before Jesus 'took' them. At the passover meal, the bread would be lifted just clear of the table and the cup raised a handsbreadth, to indicate that it was *this* bread and *this* cup which were the Passover ones. So, when the president begins to repeat the actions of Jesus at the Last Supper, he comes to the table, takes the vessels in his hands, and holds them for a moment in silence above the table before beginning the Prayer of Thanksgiving. By that action he earmarks, as it were, this particular bread and this particular wine for their Eucharistic purpose.

Series Three picks out the four-fold action of the communion with especial clarity by giving each of the four actions its own section (25, 29, 30, 33). In the 1662 rite, the taking and the breaking both came within the prayer of thanksgiving. Here they have been separated and the shape of the service is more clearly seen.

We have given the bread and the wine and the president has taken. But never let us think this means that the initiative in this service comes from us. The alms and the bread and wine are a token of the offering of ourselves, our souls and bodies, as a living sacrifice to God. But we can only offer them *to* God because we have first been given them *by* God. As the sentences in section 24 point out, all things in heaven and on earth come from him, and it is of his own gifts that we make our offering. 'We cannot, and

we dare not, offer aught of our own apart from the one
sacrifice of the Lamb of God. . . . We dare to bring bread
and wine, our work and our home life, or ourselves, only
in so far as we abase ourselves before the all-sufficiency
of the "Lamb of God that taketh away the sins of the
world".[1] Or, to put it in a homelier way, we are like little
children bringing birthday gifts to their father. He has
given them the pocket-money out of which they buy their
presents; but the gifts affirm and deepen the love between
father and son, and no father worthy the name would want
to say they were unreal gifts simply because he had provided the wherewithal for the children to buy them.

But whenever we offer back to God the things he has
first given us, he *does* things with them. We give him bread
and wine and we get back the very Body and Blood of
Jesus Christ. We give him human children in baptism and
we get back members of the Body of Christ and inheritors
of the Kingdom of Heaven. We give him our lives and we
get back life a thousandfold—life more abundant, life
which has been given and does not therefore need to be
hoarded, life over which God is in control so that we do not
need to take anxious care for bodies or food or clothing or
security or what other people think about us, life which has
become the vessel for Christ living within us.

Finally, what God gives back to us he gives us back to
use. The bread and wine are to be eaten and drunk. Baptized children are given back to their parents to be brought
up as Christians. Our lives, given to God, are given back
to us to be used in God's service. 'This is my life', I say to
God, 'it's yours'. 'This is your life', says God, 'take it
back—but use it. Have it back, to be eaten up, to be
consumed in my service.'

The bread and wine have been brought to the table. The
president has taken them. We are ready for the central
prayer of the whole rite, the Thanksgiving.

1. A. M. Ramsey, *Durham Essays and Addresses* (SPCK 1956),
p 18.

1. What is the purpose of an 'offertory procession' with alms, bread, and wine?

2. Is it necessary or desirable to present the alms at the same time as the offertory of bread and wine?

3. Ought the four actions of the Communion to be so carefully separated as they are in Series Three?

The Thanksgiving

26 The president says,

	The Lord is here.
All	**His Spirit is with us.**
President	Lift up your hearts.
All	**We lift them to the Lord.**
President	Let us give thanks to the Lord our God.
All	**It is right to give him thanks and praise.**

27 President   It is not only right, it is our duty and our joy, at all times and in all places, to give you thanks and praise, holy Father, heavenly King, almighty and eternal God, through Jesus Christ, your only Son, our Lord;

For he is your living Word; through him you have created all things from the beginning, and formed us in your own image;

Through him you have freed us from the slavery of sin, giving him to be born

as man, to die upon the cross, and
to rise again for us;

Through him you have made us a
people for your own possession,
exalting him to your right hand on high,
and sending upon us your holy and
life-giving Spirit.

28 Proper Thanksgivings.

29   Therefore with angels and archangels,
and with all the company of heaven, we
proclaim your great and glorious Name,
for ever praising you and saying:

All   **Holy, holy, holy Lord,**
God of power and might,
Heaven and earth are full of your glory.
Hosanna in the highest.

President   Accept our praises, heavenly Father,
through your Son, our Saviour Jesus
Christ; and as we follow his example
and obey his command, grant that by
the power of your Spirit these gifts
of bread and wine may be to us his
body and his blood;

For in the same night that he was
betrayed, he took bread; and after giving
you thanks, he broke it, gave it to his
disciples, and said, 'Take, eat; this is my
body which is given for you. Do this
in remembrance of me.' Again, after
supper he took the cup; he gave you
thanks, and gave it to them, saying,

'Drink this, all of you; for this is my
blood of the new Covenant, which
is shed for you and for many, for the
forgiveness of sins. Do this, as often as
you drink it, in remembrance of me.'

All **Christ has died:**
Christ is risen:
Christ will come again.

President Therefore, heavenly Father, with this
bread and this cup we do this in
remembrance of him; we celebrate and
proclaim his perfect sacrifice made once
for all upon the cross, his resurrection
from the dead, and his ascension into
heaven; and we look for his coming in
glory. Accept through him, our great high
priest, this our sacrifice of thanks and
praise; and as we eat and drink these holy
gifts in the presence of your divine
majesty, renew us by your Spirit, inspire
us with your love, and unite us in the
body of your Son, Jesus Christ our Lord.

With him, and in him, and through him,
by the power of the Holy Spirit, with
all who stand before you in earth and
heaven, we worship you, Father
Almighty, in songs of everlasting praise:

All **Blessing and honour and glory and power**
be yours for ever and ever. Amen.

Silence may be kept.

Jesus gave thanks to God over the bread and wine. Because this is what he did, we do the same as his memorial at the heart of every Holy Communion service, in the prayer of thanksgiving. To give thanks has been a characteristic of Christians from the very earliest times. Paul (1 Cor. 14. 16) writes of the plain man who is present at Christian worship being able to say 'Amen' to the giving of thanks (the Greek word is *eucharistia*) and can exhort his friends in Philippi (4. 6), 'in everything make your requests known to God in prayer and petition with *eucharistia*'. It was not long before the service of Holy Communion became known as 'the *eucharistia*'—certainly by AD 115, when Ignatius of Antioch was writing his letters to various churches on his way to martyrdom; probably even earlier.

When Jesus gave thanks at the Last Supper, it was a kind of grace at mealtime. The grace at the Passover season was a particularly significant one, bringing to mind the many acts whereby God called his chosen people, led them out of slavery, and made of them a free nation. If we wish to recall what Jesus did at that passover-tide Last Supper, we have even more for which to thank God. The Christian knows not only the God of creation and the God who made Israel into a people for his own possession, but God who sent his Son to live upon the earth, die on a cross, and rise and ascend to be our living Lord today. Similarly, just as the Jews had much to look forward to (and not least the promised Messiah) we have even more—the time when the universe in its entirety will be fully taken up into the purposes of God and he will be all in all. So our thanksgiving ranges from creation to consummation, and centres in a rehearsing once more of the words of Jesus when he commanded us to do this over the bread and the cup every time we ate and drank in memory of him.

It would be wrong to imagine any one part of the Thanksgiving to be more sacred than another. From the opening salutation to the closing *Amen*, the prayer is a unity. We cannot define within the prayer any particular moment to which we can refer as the 'moment of consecration'. Consecration is effected by thanksgiving—by the whole of the thanksgiving. Thus there are no special ceremonies associated with special parts of the prayer; the president does not take the bread and wine nor break the bread as he is reciting it. The taking has already been done (section 25) and the breaking is yet to come (section 30).

But although it is a unity, president and people each have their own part to play in it; the president in that he represents the people and has been ordained for this particular function which the Church has always reserved for the priesthood, and the people in that this is *their* Eucharist, and Eucharist cannot be celebrated by a president on his own without a supporting congregation.

The unity of this prayer should be symbolized by keeping the same posture throughout. The most appropriate attitude for thanksgiving is standing, not kneeling or crouching with head in hands. Those who are infirm or looking after small children may need to sit. There is no justification for dropping on one's knees for the narrative of institution.

This prayer, then, is a General Thanksgiving; but it is more. It is a unique prayer, which belongs nowhere else but as the centre of the Eucharist. It is the prayer in which, at his command, we remember Jesus. We can come most deeply to appreciate the significance of the Thanksgiving prayer by probing the meaning of that phrase 'we remember'. The 'we' does not refer simply to the president and the few people in church with him. It is not even the Church throughout the world, though every congregation in the Body of Christ is involved in every other congregation's Eucharist. The 'we' includes the whole Church; the Church on earth and the Church with angels, archangels, and all the company of heaven. And more; when the Eucharist is celebrated, the 'we' also includes the Lord of the Church, really present now as he was in that Upper Room when he first broke bread and shared wine and commanded his disciples to remember him by doing this. Clearly, the word 'remember' in this context means more than appears at first sight.

When Jews celebrate Passover, it is as if the act of remembrance takes them back in time so that they become the contemporaries of those who were delivered from Egyptian slavery by God's mighty act. 'It is the duty of every generation' (says a Jewish text of the second century AD) 'to think of itself as if it had personally come up out of Egypt'. A theologian recently commenting on this quotation wrote that 'the time-gap was, as it were, nullified, and these events of the past were now conceived of, not as happenings cut off in the past but as experiences shared in the present'.[1] In the act of remembrance the past is made present.

'Remembering' Jesus in the Eucharist is the same sort of thing. We do not think about him as a figure of long ago; we remember him; we re-call him; we call him out of the past and into the present. In the Eucharist the risen and living Lord is again in the midst of his people as really and as surely as he was in their midst on the first Easter Day. And the act of remembrance brings us into the presence of the whole Christ—he who was and is and is to come. 'There is also a "recalling" of the future', writes Professor Marxsen. 'The present meal is here linked with the redemptive past, and the redemptive future comes to meet those who take part in the meal.'[2] Or, as a distinguished Methodist puts it,

the history of Jesus and all that it means in its eternal consequences is appropriated by the worshippers. They remember him and it is as though they were present all the way from his cradle to his cross—and beyond. But also they grasp in advance the future kingdom, the new

1. Willi Marxsen in *Jesus in His Time*, edited by H.-J. Schultz (SPCK 1971), p 108.
2. Ibid., pp 110–11.

life in the new world of which the early Christians were so conscious.[1]

What matters, therefore, in 'remembering', is not the vividness of our imagination. The bringing of Jesus out of the past and into the present does not depend on man's efforts but on God's promise. We are not like spiritualist mediums calling up the shades of the dead, or like Aladdin commanding the genie of the lamp. When the president says 'we do this in remembrance of him', it is *God* who is in control of *us*, and not the other way round. We are taken, by the power of the Holy Spirit, into the presence of the living Jesus. We become present once again at those sacred and eternal moments of past history and are assured of our eternal destiny as we offer our lives—in our history of today—to God in union with his life.

That is why the Eucharist can be called the 'sacrament of unity'. It creates and cements the unity between God and the communicant, and thereby the unity between communicant and communicant, not only in the particular congregation gathered together in one building at one time, but between congregation and congregation in the one Body of Christ. Too often and too sadly in the past it has been a sacrament of disunity in that different rites and different forms of service and different ways of doing things in the Eucharist have separated church from church. To some extent this is understandable. The Holy Communion matters so much to Christians that those who cannot see eye to eye with each other on eucharistic doctrine have found it hard not to part company from one another. There is hope that the understanding of 'we remember' may help to reunite the broken body. Look, for example, at these recent joint statements by groups working for understanding between Churches.

---

1. Gordon S. Wakefield in *Holy Week Services* by the Joint Liturgical Group, edited by R. C. D. Jasper (SPCK and Epworth Press 1971), p 10.

The Anglican–Methodist Unity Commission gave it as their opinion that

> Holy Communion is *an act of remembrance*, 'by which, through the renewal of the corporate memory of the Church by the Holy Spirit, the great "salvation" events culminating in the Cross are re-enacted. This act of corporate recollection embraces not only the past but the future and what lies beyond history in the consummation of the kingdom of God.'[1]

In 1971, representatives of the Roman Catholic Church and of the Anglican Communion, of all shades of theological opinion from those Churches, agreed on a statement of the doctrine of the Eucharist which contained the following words:

> The notion of *memorial* as understood in the passover celebration at the time of Christ—i.e. the making effective in the present of an event in the past—has opened the way to a clearer understanding of the relationship between Christ's sacrifice and the eucharist. . . . The elements are not mere signs; Christ's body and blood become really present and are really given. But they are really present and really given in order that, receiving them, believers may be united in communion with Christ the Lord.[2]

These statements hint at some of the riches of the mystery and may help to show us why so many names have become attached to this service: 'The Lord's Supper' because we make the memorial of Jesus at his last meal with his disciples; 'The Eucharist' because it is the giving of thanks for the history of salvation and the hope of

---

1. *Anglican–Methodist Unity, 2: The Scheme* (the report of the Anglican–Methodist Unity Commission, SPCK and Epworth Press 1968) para 103.
2. *An Agreed Statement on Eucharistic Doctrine* (SPCK 1972), pp 6–8.

eternal glory; 'The Holy Communion' because in this service we are united with Christ and with each other. And yet, when all the explanation and theologizing are over, the Eucharist is *there*, like Everest, and there are countless millions of faithful Christians who would simply say, 'We do it because Christ told us to and because the Church has always obeyed this command; we cannot explain it, we can only experience it'. As Queen Elizabeth I is reported to have said,

> 'Twas God the word that spake it,
> He took the Bread and brake it;
> And what that word did make it;
> That I believe, and take it.

Here we touch the sacramental mystery of the whole universe. Mere humans are not likely to be able to plumb its depths.

With all that as prologue, we shall not need to comment much in detail on the Thanksgiving Prayer itself. It begins (section 26) with a dialogue between president and people which goes back at least as far as the third century AD. We acknowledge that God the Lord is already here, and that his Spirit, whose work it is to assist Christians in their prayers (Romans 8. 26), is with us. This is part of the paradox of the Holy Communion. It is not the summoning of an absent Lord, but the work of an ever-present God and his ever-active Spirit. The Lord is here, in the midst of his Church, enabling the Church through making Eucharist to deepen and extend the Lord's presence in and with himself. We go on to lift our hearts to where God is as we give thanks and praise to him. This is not only right, but our duty because of his command, and our joy because the service of the Lord is perfect freedom and the doing of his will the only way in which men can find true satisfaction and lasting happiness.

In the power of the Spirit and through Jesus Christ, the president gives thanks (section 27). This is appropriate at

all times and in all places because the work of God extends
to all times and all places. We go on to acknowledge that
it was through Christ his living Word that God brought
about creation and redemption, and made us a people for
his own possession. It is the Christ whom we here remember who is exalted to that Lordship which is God's, and
through him that God has sent his Spirit to give life to all
men.

Then (section 28), because there are particular times at
which the Church in its yearly cycle of recollection of all
the mysteries of the faith wishes to concentrate on one
facet of this many-splendoured jewel, the president (in
festival seasons and on saints' days) will give special thanks
for that aspect of the faith which is uppermost in the minds
of the congregation that day. The Eucharist is not a memorial of Christ's death and passion alone. Every part of the
Christian faith can have its place in the thankfulness which
is appropriate at every Eucharist.

The president (as section 29 begins) sums up thus far in
the words 'therefore with angels and archangels . . .' and
the people join in with their own ascription of praise to the
holy Lord. The people's words echo the song of the
seraphim in Isaiah 6. 3 and the words of the Palm Sunday
crowd from Matthew 21. 9; a fitting combination of the
praises of earth and heaven.

The theme of the prayer is taken up once more as, asking
God to accept our praises through his Son and to empower
them by his Spirit, the president goes on to rehearse the
events of the Last Supper. Christianity springs from what
actually happened—the historical fact of the rejection,
trial, and execution of Jesus of Nazareth. God is concerned with and implicated in our world. The president
asks that, as we follow the example of Jesus and obey his
command, the bread and wine may take to themselves the
power and the character of his body and blood, as he has
assured us they will. It is a matter not for explanation but
of experience that this *does* happen, and this solemn meal

of bread and wine becomes the sacrament of the Body and Blood of Christ.

When the narrative of institution is over, the people join in once more, with a threefold acclamation which brings past, present, and future into one focus in Christ who has died, was raised from the dead (and therefore is alive and present with us now), and will one day come again in visible power and glory. The president continues by making the act of memorial, celebrating and proclaiming Christ's sacrificial death on the Cross, resurrection, and ascension, and looking forward to the great consummation when Christ will come again.

He asks that God will 'accept this our sacrifice of thanks and praise'. A 'sacrifice' is something which has been made holy by being given over completely to God's disposal, and at the very least we can say that this is what we are doing with the thanks and praise we offer in this service. But there is more to it than this. The great fact under whose shadow all Christian worship is carried on is the one perfect and all-sufficient sacrifice made for the sins of the whole world by Jesus on the Cross. In the Eucharist we 'remember' and therefore it is as if we were present at that pivotal moment in the whole history of the relationship between God and man. We are able therefore (incredible as it may sound) through our offering of Eucharist to present once more before God that awe-ful sacrifice. In *our* sacrifice of thanks and praise it is *this* sacrifice which, although it was made once for all and can never be repeated, nevertheless we represent and re-present and renew by our remembrance and communion, and the priest through whom this is done is Christ himself (see Hebrews 9. 11f, 10. 21), for no purely human priest could do so (Hebrews 10. 11).

The prayer concludes with a solemn doxology as we worship God; *with* Jesus as our companion, *in* him as members of his Body, and *through* him because he is the channel for all our prayers to the Father. We acknowledge once more the work of the Holy Spirit in prayer and our

communion in this rite not only with God but with all who
worship him whether on earth or heaven. ('Oceans divide;
the Eucharist unites'—and this is true of all oceans,
whether the wide Pacific or the narrow black stream of
death. None can prevent eucharistic fellowship.)

The congregation add their final words of acclamation,
and their 'Amen' to the giving of thanks, which St Paul
(see 1 Cor. 14. 16 and 2 Cor. 1. 20) regarded as so essential
a way of showing that the people associated themselves
with what the president had said and done on their behalf.

The whole section has been so overwhelmingly significant that it is fitting (as the closing rubric suggests) that we
should all keep silence for a space before the eucharistic
action continues.

1. What is meant by saying that Christ is present every-
where, but especially present in the Holy Communion?

2. What is meant by calling the Holy Communion a
sacrifice?

3. How can we give *thanks* for something as dreadful as
the crucifixion of Christ?

4. Ought the president to do anything with (or make any
signs over) the bread and wine during this prayer?

The Breaking of the Bread

30 The president breaks the consecrated bread, saying:

> We break this bread
> to share in the body of Christ.

All   **Though we are many, we are one body,
because we all share in one bread.**

The third of the four actions of the Communion is that of breaking the bread. When Jesus did it at the Last Supper, the bread was simply broken in order to be shared; but it was not long before the symbolical significance of the breaking began to be perceived.

1. There is one loaf. Jesus did not share out a plateful of rolls or a bag of biscuits. There is a unity in the one loaf and all those who share it share in the unity of the one bread. When we take Communion, we do not do so as individuals, but as the Body of Christ. This is why at the breaking, we all say together (section 30), 'though we are many, we are one body, because we all share in one bread'. (1 Cor. 10. 17). If we want to make this symbolism clear, we ought to consider what kind of bread we use at the Holy Communion service. Ought it to be special 'ecclesiastical' bread, unleavened and in the form of separate wafers, looking as little as possible like the bread we see at home every day? Or is it better to use ordinary bread, baked at home or bought from the baker's, which declares the connection between our tables at home and the Lord's table, and the relevance of God to the work of our hands and our daily food, and of which a single piece can be taken and broken into as many fragments as there are communicants, showing that, many as we are, we are one body in Christ, sharing in one bread?

2. That single loaf is the result of sowing many grains of wheat. The Church, too, is made of many members. Just as the many grains have been baked into one loaf, so many members have been brought together into one Church. A very early Christian document known as the *Didaché* (a Greek word meaning 'teaching') has the following prayer for use as the piece is broken off the loaf:

> As this piece was scattered over the hills and then was brought together and made one, so let your Church be brought together from the ends of the earth into your kingdom.

Many as we are, we become part of one body in Christ.

3. The bread is broken; it is Christ's body. We cannot
help seeing deep symbolism here, too. The day after he
broke the bread in the Upper Room, his flesh was broken
open on the cross. Before the work of Christ could be
finished, before he could be of use to us, his body had to be
broken. Again and again in this service of Holy Communion, our thoughts keep returning to the Cross of Jesus.
A Christianity without the Cross is no Christianity at all.
Jesus is the 'Bread of the world in mercy broken, Wine of
the soul in mercy shed', and this feast is 'to us the token
that by [his] grace our souls are fed'.

We who are Christians need to take that truth into our
own lives.

> Our wills are ours, we know not how;
> Our wills are ours, to make them Thine.

Unless we are 'broken in', unless our wills are ours but
made his, we are of little use to Christ. The freedom of a
colt is a beautiful thing, but a horse which has been broken
in is of far greater beauty and use. Self-centredness, self-
will, has to be curbed, broken, made over to God if God is
to use a person in his service. When we take the broken
bread into our bodies at Holy Communion, this can be
one of the thoughts passing through our minds.

---

1. What kind of bread is best for breaking conveniently
and meaningfully in the sight of the congregation?

2. Is the breaking of the bread utilitarian or symbolical?
Or can it be both?

The Giving of the Bread and the Cup

31 President   As our Saviour has taught us,
so we pray:

All   **Our Father in heaven,
hallowed be your Name,
your kingdom come,
your will be done,
on earth as in heaven.
Give us today our daily bread.
Forgive us our sins
as we forgive those who sin against us.
Do not bring us to the time of trial
but deliver us from evil.**

**For the kingdom, the power, and the
glory are yours
now and for ever. Amen.**

32 President   Draw near with faith. Receive the body
of our Lord Jesus Christ which he gave
for you, and his blood which he shed
for you. Remember that he died for you,
and feed on him in your hearts by faith
with thanksgiving.

33 The president and the other communicants receive the
holy communion.

At the administration the ministers say to each
communicant

The Body of Christ keep you
in eternal life.

The Blood of Christ keep you
in eternal life.

The communicant replies each time,

Amen.

and then receives.

34 During THE COMMUNION these and other hymns
and anthems may be sung:

**Blessed is he who comes in the name
of the Lord. Hosanna in the highest.**

**Jesus, Lamb of God: have mercy on us.
Jesus, bearer of our sins: have mercy
on us.
Jesus, redeemer of the world: give us
your peace.**

35 If either or both of the consecrated elements are likely
to prove insufficient, the president returns to the holy
table and adds more, with these words:

Having given thanks to you, Father,
over the bread and the cup according
to the institution of your Son, Jesus
Christ, who said, 'Take, eat; this is my
body', (and/or 'Drink this, this is my
blood') we pray that this bread/wine
also may be to us his body/blood and
be received in remembrance of him.

36 Any consecrated bread and wine which is not required
for purposes of communion is consumed at the end of
the administration, or after the service.

Sharing is at the heart of the Holy Communion. God shares his gift of Jesus Christ among us, and we are about to share the bread and the cup with the whole congregation of the faithful. We approach the gift of Jesus with the words of Jesus on our lips, speaking to God as our Father because his own Son taught us to do so. The genius of the Lord's Prayer is that it is appropriate at so many times and in so many different situations, and each time it takes its particular colouring from the context within which it is used. Here our thoughts will probably be on the phrase about 'daily bread', as we ask God to give us today the Bread of Life and to come inside us to forgive us all our sins.

Jesus taught us to pray 'after this manner', and we shall be wise to take the pattern of this prayer as the pattern of all prayer. It begins with God, our Father, in heaven. Prayer begins in the quiet unhurried contemplation of the Object of prayer. When we pray, we do not burst in with ourselves and our desires or our fears or our sins. First we look towards God, in wonderful majesty, and we worship.

Then come three petitions. But they are Godward petitions, concerned with his Name, his kingdom, and his will. Christian prayer starts by looking towards God and continues by putting as its first priorities what God wants. God's Name is hallowed, his kingdom has come, and his will is done in heaven. The rub comes when 'on earth' is prefixed to 'as in heaven'. Here, in a sinful and fallen universe, it is not so easy to do God's will, and we see the point of these petitions immediately.

The first things for which we pray had a Godward bearing. Now we can come down to our own needs. The prayer asks only for the most basic—food, forgiveness, protection. But, in so doing, it is amazingly comprehensive and sends our prayers towards every aspect of life and the whole of the being of God. Food reminds us of God the Father, maker of heaven and earth; forgiveness sends us to God the Son, who died upon the Cross for the sin of the

whole world; help and deliverance come from God the
Holy Spirit, who is about the path of every Christian to
empower him in his daily living. It puts under the protection of God the Holy Trinity our bodies which need food,
our minds which need guiding, and our souls which need
forgiveness; and it speaks of the past which needs absolution, the present which calls for nourishment, and the
future which calls for guidance.

Notice, too (as we said on page 19 above) that the place
for our sins to be dealt with is not at the beginning of our
prayer, but only when we have been so touched with the
glory of our heavenly Father and the holiness of his Name
that we realize more genuinely and more fully our need
for pardon.

We ask for our sins to be forgiven as we forgive those
who sin against us. Not that we can *earn* forgiveness by
being forgiving, or that we can only expect as much forgiveness from God as we exercise towards others. Had
that been so, we would be of all men most miserable, for do
we not remember the story Jesus told (Matt. 18. 23–35) of
the comparison between our debt towards God which runs
into millions and what we are owed by our fellow-men?
No; this part of the prayer is an indication that only those
who know how to forgive know what forgiveness is, and
those who do not know what forgiveness is, cannot receive
it from God.

'Do not bring us to the time of trial', we pray. But 'no
one under trial or temptation should say, "I am being
tempted by God"; for God is untouched by evil, and does
not himself tempt anyone. Temptation arises when a man
is enticed and lured away by his own lust' (James 1. 13f).
Nobody should go looking for temptation; we should all
pray that we be spared the trial as much as possible,
because we know our own frailty. Evil is pernicious and
will not easily be repelled, and our prayer is for deliverance
from its recurrent power.

But the prayer cannot end on so negative a note. Having

begun with God and circled downwards from heaven to earth, and then from our needs to our sins, and thence to that ultimate evil from which we seek deliverance, we complete the circle back again and end with an ascription to God, whose kingdom, power, and glory are present and enduring realities. Prayer may include everything in heaven, on the earth, and under the earth; but it begins in God and it returns to God, for it is wholly concerned with God.

When the Lord's Prayer has been said, the president (section 32) invites the people to come round and share at the Lord's table in the Lord's feast. The essence of a meal is friendship, friendliness, sharing. When people have to eat alone, we feel sorry for them because we know that meals ought not to be like that. Nor ought this meal of the Eucharist. The bread and the cup are given to us individually, but what we are offered is a meal which we all share with each other, as a family. Together, we enjoy our companionship round the table of the Lord. This is an individual gift shared in a family setting.

We are bidden (section 32) to remember Christ's death which makes this Eucharist possible, and to feed on him in our hearts by faith with thanksgiving. As St Paul said (1 Cor. 11. 26), 'every time you eat this bread and drink this cup, you proclaim the death of the Lord until he comes'. One day we shall see Christ face to face and then there will be no need of sacraments. But until that day comes, we show forth Jesus in his death and his life through the bread we eat and the wine we drink.

The communion of president, assistants, and congregation follows (section 33). The words of invitation in the preceding section provide a doctrinal back-cloth against which the act of reception is set, and the president should not receive his communion until after they have been said. That would be to separate president from people at the moment when they should be seen to be all alike before God, all equally guests at the table whose host is God. If the people wish to, they may save time by coming up and placing themselves around the table whilst the president and his assistants are communicating; or there is no reason why they should not receive first and let the president's own communion follow.

The people may receive standing or kneeling. In many churches, children and other people who may be unconfirmed or unready to receive the elements are invited to come up to the table for a verbal blessing instead of the blessing which comes with the bread and wine.

At the administration (section 33) the ministers say a short prayer as they come to each communicant.[1] The first half of the 1662 form of administration was a prayer, but the communicant did not say his 'Amen' to it. In series Two, there was an 'Amen', but it was not in response to a prayer. Here, the communicants are treated as individuals, and each one says his 'so be it' to the minister's prayer before receiving the Body or the Blood of Christ which keeps him in eternal life. Eternal life is not something for which we have to wait until the world to come (see the words of the absolution in section 19); it is a present possession of the Christian who, already in this life, is in the heavenly places with Christ Jesus. He who eats the Bread of life is kept in the life eternal.

So the Body of Christ assembled for the Eucharist—a body of such diverse members—comes to the table of Christ to receive the Body of Christ; to receive what it already is, to become what it has already declared itself to be; and to return from the altar to the world bearing the Body within it to the world which needs it.

While this is happening, hymns and anthems may be sung. Two traditional ones are given in section 34; but if there is to be any music here, it need not be limited to these items.

---

1. This will be the case if the Series Three words are used. Permission is given in the introductory notes to use the forms authorized in Second Series at this point if they are preferred, at least during the initial period of experimental use of the service.

Two rubrics (35 and 36) round off this division of the service. The first tells the president what to do if the bread or the wine look likely to run out before all the people have communicated. He should return to the table and add more to what remains, using a form of words which makes explicit what he is doing. There is no need to repeat all or part of the Thanksgiving Prayer—the prayer does not effect any magical change in the elements over which it is said. It is the whole eucharistic action which sets apart bread and wine to be for us Christ's body and blood and it is therefore sufficient that the president should return to the table and acknowledge this in a suitable way.

The final rubric (36) points out that the bread and wine have been set aside for purposes of communion and for no other reason. Some may be needed for those who, although part of the congregation, are prevented through sickness from being in church. To take the consecrated bread and wine (either immediately after the service or even some days later) to the sick tells them that they are still part of the unity of the Body of Christ and share in the same one bread and one cup as their healthy brothers and sisters in Christ. But the rest of the bread and wine remaining is consumed either at the end of the administration or after the service, lest people get the mistaken idea that what has served as the vehicle for Christ's presence within the eucharistic action should possess of itself, and apart from the Eucharist, any greater significance than any other piece of bread or cup of wine.

1. Why do you think the Lord's Prayer has been placed at this particular point of the service?

2. Does it matter whether you receive the Communion standing or kneeling?

3. Should the people receive their Communion in silence or to musical accompaniment?

After Communion

37 A seasonal sentence may be said.
    Silence may be kept.

38 Either or both of the following prayers are said:

39 President   Father of all, we give you thanks and
                 praise, that when we were still far off
                 you met us in your Son and brought us
                 home. Dying and living, he declared
                 your love, gave us grace, and opened
                 the gate of glory. May we who share
                 Christ's body live his risen life; we who
                 drink his cup bring life to others; we
                 whom the Spirit lights give light to the
                 world. Keep us in this hope that we
                 have grasped; so we and all your chil-
                 dren shall be free, and the whole earth
                 live to praise your Name; through
                 Christ our Lord.

     All   **Amen.**

40 All   **Almighty God,**
                 we thank you for feeding us
                 with the body and blood of your Son
                 **   Jesus Christ.**
                 Through him we offer you
                 **   our souls and bodies**
                 to be a living sacrifice.
                 Send us out
                 in the power of your Spirit
                 to live and work
                 to your praise and glory. Amen.

41 A hymn or canticle may be sung.

42 The president may say this or the appropriate seasonal
blessing.

> The peace of God, which passes all
> understanding, keep your hearts and
> minds in the knowledge and love of
> God, and of his Son Jesus Christ our
> Lord;

> And the blessing of God Almighty,
> the Father, the Son, and the Holy
> Spirit, be among you, and remain with
> you always.

All   **Amen.**

43 President   Go in peace and serve the Lord.

All   **In the name of Christ. Amen.**

44 The Ministers and people depart.

45 Seasonal Blessings.

The climax is over. As in all good drama, there is very little
left to do or say. There simply follows one or both of two
prayers (sections 39 and 40), and the president then dis-
misses the people in peace to serve the Lord (43). Of the
two prayers, one is for the president alone to use and the
other is for the congregation to join in. The president's
prayer (39) thanks God for being like the father of the
Prodigal Son, who met him when he was far off and
brought him home; and expresses the hope that we may
bring the life and light of the Eucharist into a dead, dark
world, and in our freedom as sons of a heavenly Father,
help all the earth to live to the praise of God's Name. The
other prayer (40) is a brief one in which the congregation
thanks God for what he has done, offers itself for his

service, and prays to be sent out to live and work to his praíse and glory. The note on which the service ends is that word 'peace' (*shalom*), the greeting so often on the lips of Jesus, in which the congregation is bidden to go out intending to make that peace effective outside the church walls (43).

Other elements may be added, so long as they do not blunt the dramatic impact of the shape of the service by making the post-communion over-long. Immediately after the communion of the people, there can be a sentence (section 37) reminding them of the season of the Church's year or the particular occasion within which this Eucharist has been set; and there can with advantage be a period of silence for thankful recollection.

Between the final prayer and the dismissal, there may be a hymn or a canticle (41) and a blessing—either a standard one (42) or a special one for the season (45). Strictly speaking, this is unnecessary, for we can receive no greater blessing than the indwelling eucharistic presence of Jesus Christ, and a verbal blessing can add nothing to this. But most congregations are not so severely logical, and will probably feel that it fitly rounds off the service to hear the president wish that God's peace should keep guard over their hearts and minds and that God's blessing should be among them and remain with them.

Whether or not there is a blessing, however, the inevitable last words should be the dismissal; those dangerous words which send the followers of Jesus out from the safety of the Lord's table, out from the gathering where all are followers of the Lord Jesus, into the hostile or uninterested world, where it is not so easy to stand firm or serve the Lord.

After the Last Supper, Jesus and the disciples left the Upper Room. One of them left, having made up his mind to help hand Jesus over to his enemies. One left, determined not to deny him, and found that his resolution melted away within hours. One was to keep watch with the women at the Cross; one was to be incredulous on the evening of the third day; many of them were to leave no visible mark on the pages of history.

Yet despite their failures, their weaknesses, and their sin, to those who could come back to the Risen Jesus and say, 'I want to go in peace and serve the Lord', he came in the power of the Holy Spirit so that they could go out to turn the world upside down and be known as the people who had been with Jesus (Acts 17. 6, 4. 13). His last words on earth, spoken on the Mount of the Ascension, were promise and challenge combined: 'You will receive power when the Holy Spirit comes upon you; and you will bear witness for me in Jerusalem, and all over Judea and Samaria, and away to the ends of the earth' (Acts 1. 8). His followers soon discovered the power which made that promise come true.

God grant that we may never be like Judas as we leave the Lord's table. But if we are Peters or Johns or Thomases —or as obscure as Thaddaeus or Simon the Zealot—God can send us out with the Spirit of his Son within us, and command us to make him known wherever we go. Christ has no hands but ours, no feet but ours, no lips but ours, no eyes but ours, no life but his own, living within us to do his work in the world. At Pentecost, the Spirit came like wind and fire. His touch has still that ancient power—if we have the courage to let go, and let him take control of our lives.

Jesus came into the world at Bethlehem. He will come again in glory at the end of time. But before that great Last Day, he comes to hearts who are ready to receive him, and through those hearts to the world he longs to make his own. In the Eucharist, Christ comes to his own, so that his own may present him before the world.

Even so, come, Lord Jesus!

---

1. Ought there to be a blessing at the end of the service?

2. Does it help you in your worship to use a service clearly divided so that the pattern of the rite stands out?

3. What is the relation between the Eucharist and the daily life of the Christian?

For Further Reading

The history of Anglican worship from the beginnings up to Second Series is briefly told in D. E. W. Harrison's book *Common Prayer in the Church of England* (SPCK; revised edition 1969). For background to the texts used in Series Three, see *Modern Liturgical Texts* by the Church of England Liturgical Commission (SPCK 1968) and *Prayers We Have In Common* by the International Consultation on English Texts (Geoffrey Chapman 1970). The Church of England Liturgical Commission has produced its official *Commentary on Holy Communion Series Three* (SPCK 1971) which assumes some degree of theological and liturgical knowledge in its readers, whilst a joint working party of the Church of England Liturgical Commission and the Council for the Care of Churches has issued an illustrated booklet called *The Presentation of the Eucharist* (SPCK 1971) containing some commentary and suggestions as to the ordering of the service.

Readers who want a commentary on the Nicene Creed will be admirably served by John Burnaby's book *The Belief of Christendom* (NS and SPCK 1959); and, for the Our Father, they are advised to read *The Lord's Prayer* by C. F. Evans (SPCK 1963).